I am invisible,

I walk around and no one sees me.

I make noise,

And no one hears.

I write words,

But no one read them.

I am but a single star,

Floating amongst millions

And yet I seem to be oblivious

To all who point their telescopes upward.

Is this what it's like to be alone?

Is this what it feels like to be part of

Humanity,

Yet not?

I am a rose

Whose petals fold when the rain falls.

I am a sailing ship, casting out lines

That no one will ever reach.

I am a shadow

Passing through rays of sunlight.

I am a stray cat,

Wandering through alleys,

Travelling much trodden pathways,

Searching for a place to belong

A Dreamer's Wings

White dove, be still, silent

Awake with me from a pleasant dream,

And enter my world.

Whisper softly,

Tell me there's nothing to fear.

Endlessly I write words

I don't believe.

I am trapped within myself,

Like the caged dove

Longing to fly.

Immortality is far beyond my reach

My hopes and dreams, caught,

Suspended in time.

Fly far, little dove,

Soar away

You have your freedom.

I will, too,

Someday.

Little dove, you don't need anything

You have found true happiness.

Help me search, so that one day,

I might find it too.

Lost Time
(for Grm. T.)

Because I am older,

I don't like to visit.

You talk for hours…

I never know how to get away.

Now, I'm afraid I'll forget the sound of your voice.

Perhaps, you are lonely

As you must be now,

Abed in room 350

After being poked and prodded

By aliens in white gowns—

Not the kind of company

You expected to keep tonight.

My father's voice is soft, almost distant.

"She's a tough old bird," he says, "but,

There's no cure for what she has.

We can't stop the inevitable."

How do you say *I'm sorry*

To someone whose tomorrow

Is not certain?

How do you say *good-bye*

To twice-told tales

Or poems,

Scratched on a memo pad?

How do you

Forgive yourself?

Winter Roses

Close your eyes;

Dreams are for remembering…

In the darkness they found you

Shivering, anxious, alone;

They took you in.

Without a thought

You forfeited your soul

In exchange for acceptance,

Hung it up to forget

Who you were…

Who you might have become.

You remember now,

The raw, life-rendering flesh,

Pink and boiling in brine.

You recall the caravans

Of sun-bleached skeletons

Clattering in the breeze,

Their song of hunger

Echoing in your ears

And the scarlet marrow,

Sweet,

Like honey on your tongue.

Each time you fed

The acid rose in your throat

And you purged yourself

Of the evil—

A flicker of the soul

That once was,

Remained.

It kept you alive.

Visions torment your fragile mind;

Visions as dark and fathomless as the night.

You see again,

Purple smoke rising,

Shadows of the living.

Intoxicated with fear,

You choke back violent tears.

You know.

You know now they feed you

To sustain themselves.

Run…

Snatch your soul and run

Never look back

Seek redemption

Filter your past

Through a honey-combed heart

Reach for the soft, amber pitch

To bind with viscous strength

Body and soul

Look up—

The snow still falls like Gypsophila

Bespeckled with dew;

Pearls of human existence

Blown softly

Through the ages,

Transcending time

In white, rushing waves.

In a kaleidoscope of color,

The snowflakes burst

Into beads of blue glass

Hung high upon a

Tern-guarded steeple,

Throwing rainbows

Against a shimmering white wall

And all around you,

Winter Roses,

Throbbing with life;

Their pale faces radiant

Like heavenly stars

Cast upon the earth

To shelter you,

Until you wake.

These are your memories;

Open your eyes

And move on

The Vigil

I wonder what you dream

When you close your eyes?

Do you think of spring

And the garden

You'll never plant?

Do you think about all you never did,

The places you'll never see?

Do you think of me?

Sometimes,

I wonder if I'm dreaming.

Perhaps,

This is all a nightmare;

A hideous dream

That will end

As soon as it begins.

I find myself walking

Through nights gone past;

The Snow Moon

Shedding its somber light

Across a well-worn path,

And God's canopy

Holding us close

Like flecks of windswept diamond

Through heaven's tears

I fly;

With wings,

Move silently

Among feathered Gypsophila petals

Then rest quietly

On soft pillows of serenity.

Broken reverie:

    A sigh of sadness

    A hint of tears

    Afraid to sleep,

    Knowing dreams are just that

Nothing lasts forever

The thread wears thin
As Irish lace.
Your dance diminishes,
Your Tree of Life unravels,
Falling in endless lacy folds
Upon the earth.

Yesterday,
I caught a glimpse,
Of the path you must follow.
God's blade
Sliced through the dark clouds of pain,
Letting bright rays of love-light
Shimmer in.

Brave heart!
To walk the path alone.
I can only hope as much
When my thread severs,
Drawing me close toward eternity.

Ceremony:

A Journey

(for my father)

Eighteen:

Fresh out of high school

And clueless about the future

Enlist:

173rd Airborne Brigade

Vietnam: 1967-1968

One tour of torture.

Humping through the jungle in the rain,

Parachuting with an eighty pound sack,

A wound to the hand from an ally gun,

Malaria's Fever: Brush with Death.

Born to live,

Fight, while others die around you.

Anxious to return,

Letters home signed,

"Your number two son."

Return, War Vet;

Purple Heart, Bronze Star.

Forget, move on,

Make new memories to erase the old.

Twenty-six years,

A ceremonial calm.

Called back,

Fighting again,

To serve, protect:

The V.A.

School Administration

Suburbane Propane

Reliving the past moment by moment.

Thirty books in a black crate

Written by other survivors.

A five volume documentary

Narrated by Walter Cronkite.

Places, names, emotions,

Meaningless to me;

The end of a long and difficult journey for you.

Or maybe it's just another pause

In the ceremony.

Reflection

Shards of silver light:

Reflections through a pane of glass…

Are these my hands

Moving across the page?

I feel the pen between my fingers

I see the ink,

Thick and black,

Filling in the spaces

Yet, where are the words?

What are these images I see?

Reflections…of me?

Is this my face

A pale, dim star?

Are these my eyes,

These shy, sapphire sparks?

What of these tears?

The dreams…of my heart?

Where *do* dreams go

When I cannot close my eyes,

When my heart is torn

And bleeds…

The night is full of wanderers,

Seekers of the dreams

That hide in the shadows,

Concealed by the light

If I were to search hard enough,

With my night-worn eyes,

Would I find them?

Would I find my dreams?

Could I gather them close

In my arms?

My hand moves

Across the page

And the ink falls in clots

Too thick for thoughts or words,

Images without form and meaning…

Or is it just another reflection?

River Dreams

I feel cold,

Like glass

When river dreams return,

When my flaming heart burns like ice.

Can this be love?

This wonder

That sends the night

Into a concert of stars

Full of dark music

And avenues that

Run deep

With unspoken words?

When our lips touch,

I ignite with the sordid

Pleasures of life—

I search for water

To cool this flame I feel

As we walk

Beneath bridges

Run,

As the music fades

Blending with your whispered words

That pound against my ears

Like waves…

Comfort me,

When river dreams leave,

Flow from my heart

Like the deep red life of the departed.

Kiss me again

When river dreams die,

When the stars cascade from the heaven,

Vanish behind saffron rays of light…

Time

Time weathers like most things

Like passing stars that scrape

The skyline

Leaving scars…

After dark, river smoke rushes

Cold through my dreams,

A gray, drunken melody scattering notes

Like rain

I shiver

Feeling night fall

Run

Wanting to crush the noise

The music

Eating my days like apples

I must get to the bridge

Before light,

Before the unusual shine of sun,

Before the expensive smell of city perfume

Takes you away,

Buries you beneath avenues

Of life stealing architecture

Breathe…heart beating,

Staring down at the inky swirls

Of polluted water..

Time weathers like most things,

Though never fast enough

My Dream

We meet in the usual way—

In a secluded wood,

Among my roses,

Beneath the moonlight…

If I want to be creative,

Feel like a journey through time,

It may be that I find you in a prairie cabin,

Among France's white crosses in the heat of war,

Within the embrace of a Highland fortress…

      It is a dream, after all.

      My dream.

I've never seen your face,

But does that matter?

You're my tall, handsome stranger

Who is willing to take a chance

On this shy flower.

I know you by many names:

From books

Movies

The latest television show

Yet, you never change.

I wonder how God sets our paths to meet

How our eyes seek each other across time.

You take my hand and we dance…

After the music fades

You linger…

I haven't much to say,

Speaking silently with my eyes;

You speak instead,

Selecting the words you will say

To let me hear your thoughts,

To allow your heart to be known.

And what of my heart?

You know it already.

I have never lived

But in dreams.

So, how can I feel the first kiss,

Warm, like dawn's blush,

Your lips gently exploring mine?

Or, hear your soft laughter as I pull away,

Awkward, gasping from inexperience?

How can I feel your embrace,

Your body close to mine,

Hands resting on my back

As your kiss deepens,

Devouring me?

How can I say *I love you* to a dream?

When alone you take my hand,

Whispering my name

As you place on my finger

The pearl,

Your love,

Your soul

Glistening like tears

Kissed and given freely by God!

Can I say *I love yo*u

Can I believe

When the music escorts me to your side,

As you promise forever

Your love,

Your heart,

Eternity?

Can I say *I love yo*u

Our first night

With moonlight falling across the bed

Where a thousand crimson petals lay

To cradle me?

My heart yearns for what you're asking

Yet my mind plays with excuses,

Fears of not knowing,

Fleeting innocence,

Shattering the dream…

How can I feel your breath quicken

As you come to me,

Eyes holding mine?

How can I feel the heat flush my face

At your nakedness,

At your muscled beauty,

At your body's desire…

How can I feel the trembling of your hand

As it reaches for me,

Draws me to your kiss,

Liquid, like this dream?

How can I feel your fingers

Slipping the gown over my shoulders

So it tumbles to the floor,

So I stand before you

Pale and tremulous?

How can I feel you lifting me in your arms

Or feel my breasts,

Warmly pressed against your chest

Or the way you lower me to the bed,

Your body atop mine,

Protecting,

Loving…

How can I fell my heart

Throbbing at your touch,

Your fingers caressing each curve,

Every hollow,

Your lips kissing my fragility

Melting my soul?

How can I feel the moment of our joining,

My fingers curling at your fullness consuming me,

The slight pain of the first time

Swiftly forgotten

As I struggle to deepen your desire

So it might remain forever in my core;

A vibrating melody

Forever dancing within…

How can I hear your pensive sigh

Mingling with my own

As we part,

Kiss again,

Lingering in each other's arms?

How can I feel your love

When I'm too tired to whisper

What's in my heart,

Too tired to kiss once more,

Too tired even,

To sustain my dream…

I can feel the sun's rays

Warm, like a half-remembered kiss,

My body damp, glistening with love's heat.

I can feel myself waking alone,

No lover at my side,

An empty space

That once was filled…

I can feel

Fragments of a dream

Piercing,

And the heart's lonely tears

Spilling from my eyes…

My Psalm

Let me sing

The words of my heart

The longings of my soul

Lord, gather 'round the

This mortal frame

Take up the fight

And lead me, guide me

Through darkness

Through tears

That flood h my eyes

With pain.

Take my hand,

Lead,

Usher me toward dawn

Your peace

Gathering like waves,

Cradling Your perfect pearl—

My heavenly soul…

Let me rest here awhile

In Your arms…

Silences

You summon me from flight,

Voice shattering my weariness

With wonder—

The echo of memory held fast

By unrequited dreams

You call to me from loneliness,

Heart not recognizing past blessing—

Forgotten

In the solitude of seasons.

The trickery of twilight

Dispels reason

Til reassurance trembles my soul

Recalling, as you pass above,

The silhouette of my visions

Arise from slumber

To the caress of currents

On awkward wings

Made lovely in

Shadowed flight,

To the soft hush,

The whisper of feathers

Against my up-turned face

To the lilt of wind song

Deep in the night's silences

Silence, save the calling,

The gasp of my heart

As you fade,

Solitary, though no longer alone…

I sigh with the thrill of promise

As through the veil of tears

I embrace a mingling of souls

The majesty of love

Casting truth from my longings

Emergence

Soon the brown earth must breathe

Quiet life coaxed sweetly from

Winter sanctuary

The tranquil murmur of

Fresh Spring-Song

Struggles to emerge

Through the stone shell of frost

Roots explode

Through their moist condition

As clouds burst softly

Ripe with rain

Sprouts rustle

Beneath mossy blankets

Rising from a long protective night

Where no light fell wild upon fertile blooms

And death grew heavy as

Morning wilted to twilight

Come here my love,

Leave the long night to wither

Let every summer shade

Thrive in this

Flowery Eden

Breathe in the cloud of life

Winding soft and peaceful through this dawn

Sweet tendril song emerges

Green above the earth

Listen to the murmur of light

Tranquil on our path

Fresh blossoms rain with sun

Fall heavy as night

On this sanctuary

Where the flower of spring

Explodes from winter's withering hand

The Wait

She withers with longing
For secret days
Fresh frost forming a soft protection
Like moss blanketing
Her summer vine

She waits in ripe anticipation
For peaceful storms
Heavily raining their bouquet
Like fertile showers that once
Moistened her secret sorrow

She dies,
Dreaming of his love
Breathing sunlight
Through her shadows
The bliss of morning
A murmur in the emerging night

She listens and slumber comes
Climbing between seasons

In sweet explosion

Asleep in the earth

Her tendrils still,

Frozen in eternity…

The sun shines in secret for him

Giving breath to his quiet longing

His morning,

His wild struggle for life

He rustles,

Soft with song and wind

Coaxing spring from every stone

The peace of death

Lifting with shadow

Climbing through darkness

To light

Come listen to the heavy murmur

Tranquil beneath cloud and vine

Left lifeless with hope

Though harsh and wild were

The paths

How sweet her love

Chill winter's past

Dying to this Eden

Driving days from

His long seclusion

The Lesson

Teach him through fear

That he would find life

Between truth and dreams

Inspire his soul to live

As her hero

Let full the heart's wisdom speak

Time haunts

In words

She gives voice to love

Takes from another the desire to fight

Answers the spirit's quest of wonder

To discover courage

When hope is but a whisper

Upon the wind

Empty words that

Turn to longing

In the escape of fear,

Enter death

To find his end

As her hero

The heart of love

Opens a world

In which

The soul can begin to live

Come dance

If only to linger

Remember his embrace

Voice soft,

Broken breath,

Velvet with the fire of longing

He listens for her trust

Above the rhythm of her heart

Learning the child's song

Of innocence

He knows

Eternity

Though young is the heart

That speaks;

Every kiss

Awakening stars

Freeing ghosts of their night web

Blazing to the healing joy of morning

How brilliant the cloud!

How vast the poetry of man

From his God!

When by magic

Peace flowers the change

Casting deep from His hand

The soul…

She haunts him

Surrounding like words…

Would he never forsake his angel;

Would he always have life

And her love

Beyond Dreams

This dream is

Too empty of life—

I search for words to write

A voice to speak

Discovering only fear

Each time,

So far from truth

Wandering where whispers haunt

Almost finding, yet never reaching

The answers

Another night spent hoping,

Heart longing to begin,

To emerge from this strange

Inspired world

Whole and alive

Desire exploding

Full of mystery

Strange wisdom

Above me

Like the birth of stars

Ripe with the magic of

The Heavens at their core

Love,

Still beat of the soul

Peace against my breast

As the moonlight

In lovely tenderness

Embraces my heart

Spilling forth to reach

Beyond my dreams

Standing Still

Standing still on a Solstice morn

Caught in the stillness

Between night and dawn

In the hush

Where only your heart beat is heard

A steady throb against my cheek

Counting the moments that linger

Like butterflies over a nectared bloom…

Solstice morning

Standing still

So I might treasure your embrace

Long after the daylight fades to another night

And the moon circles 'round

Like your arms

Like your lips upon mine

Full and deep

Tasting of springtime

And cherry blossoms

Pink and white with hope

The shortest day sets

Into the longest night

Dancing with stars

With snowflakes

Chilling the skin

Like the shivers of your love

Darting like winter birds

Across the frozen landscape

Across my moon-kissed body…

I scarcely breath at your welcomed touch

In the night's velvet silence

Love's warmth comforting,

Pleasuring,

Through the year's longest night…

Heart Song

Joy—

Like sunshine

Scattered across a summer meadow

Be-jeweled of dew

Happiness—

Aroused like

Sleepy bees

Humming to their task

Gathering the sweetness of clover

Life

Wonder—

Fluttering freely

In a heavenly tumult

Of butterflies

Dancing, pulsating, beating

With the gentle throb of life

Love—

Gently resting

Against my breast

As a dove come home

To the safety of her nest

My heart alive with the thrill

Of its closeness

Of the reality

The wonder

The happiness

The joy

The encompassing calm

Like a summer breeze

Caressing my cheek

A stolen kiss

A touch…

I am lost

In a soul-touching

Moment

Lost,

Yet found

Found in your reflection

Found in your embrace

Found in your heart

Found,

In your love

Staying

The impression of my head remains

Upon your pillow

The rumpled comforter

Twisted from my body

Like a Monarch freeing herself

From a warm chrysalis

I linger,

Not wanting to leave you alone

The longing in your eyes

For my comfort

My love to hold

Through the cold winter night

Saddens me

Tears at me…

Caught,

Like a butterfly

In a spider's web

Struggling with new wings

To escape

The restrictions surrounding me

And those fluttery ones within

I'll return,

My love,

Tonight

For awhile

Tonight

Perhaps,

To stay

Wanting You

Stolen kiss

At twilight

Just a touch

Brushing the wisps of hair

From my cheek

My forehead rests

Against yours

Fingers twisted

Heart throbbing

Longing again

For the taste of

Your lips,

Your touch,

Gentle,

Electrifying,

Sparking,

Like the stars

In your eyes…

Wanting you,

Though afraid;

To love again

To trust

To fly…

Wanting you,

As your lips seek mine again

In the darkness.

Whispered assurance

Whispered promises

Whispered love…

The Dance

I'd slipped away

But a moment

Leaving you alone

Amidst the crowd

Leaving you to idle chatter

And a meal growing cold in my absence

Stepping from the church

Winding my way across

The lawn

I caught your gaze,

Your anticipation

My pace quickens

As does my heart

At the smile

Creasing your lips

Your outstretched hand

Grasping my own

Drawing me into

A dance

Your lips moving

In song

While the crowd stares

At happiness

And a love

That shadows

Even the sunlight

On a chill September

Afternoon

Colliding

This evening
As we read
You professed
Your love
In promises
Heaven-breathed
Heart-spoken
Repeated in a whisper
By my soul

In your eyes,
A sparkle—
Gold-flecked hope
Of a man's desire.

A touch to my cheek,
The taste of your lips upon mine
Electrifies—
My heart sparking,
Pounding
As you draw me up

Into your embrace

Your fingers

Ignite my nakedness

Chilling me

Til I'm wrapped up

Warmly by your arms

My legs encircling you.

Softly,

With love on your lips

You ask,

Ask...

Yes, my husband,

Yes,

And for a moment,

All inhibitions lost,

We are one—

One in love,

One in life,

One in song

A simple aria

Encircling,

Like your arms,

My legs…

I dampen

From your loving—

Your name

Escapes my lips

As you caress

My petals

Coaxing them to bloom

Soon,

Like colliding stars,

We explode

You and I

Like sunshine penetrating

The clouds

In a swirl of shimmering light.

My breath vanishes

Like vapor

My body tenses,

Heightened in the

Merging of souls

A moment

And breath returns.

I collapse in

A concentrated sigh

Of peace

Against your chest,

Your heartbeat

Thrumming in my ear…

And I dream

Of colliding—

Two stars

Becoming one

Heartbeat

(for my husband)

Twilight

And we're alone

Slipping naked

Into the silky darkness

Soft like the

Touch of yours lips
Brushing across my cheek.

Your hand gropes for mine
Drawing it to your face
My fingers trailing your jaw
Til I feel the tickle of your tongue
Exploring, tasting…

I laugh,
Reclaiming my hand
Cuddling close,
Squishing my body
As far against yours as possible.

I sigh,
Looking up into the
Gold-flecked sparkle
Of your eyes
Meeting my reflection…
And I turn away
Feeling awkward,
Shivering as a night breeze

Travels across my

Moon-glossed skin

While your arm slips about me,

The heat of your damp body

Warming me,

Chilling me…

I glance at you again—

You wink,

I blush

Dipping my head

Studying the uncaged tiger

Leaping from your forearm—

Slowly, you lift my chin

Gazing into the marbled blue

Of my eyes.

Leaning near

Your lips brush over mine

Once,

Then again

As I slip into your

Passionate embrace…

Stillness

But a moment—

A moment

Where there's naught save

The hush of breath,

The whisper of a name,

My lover's heart beat

In rhythm with my own

As our bodies merge

In the harmony of

A song…

Talk to Me

I saw you sitting

Cool and relaxed

On a late summer morn

You were talking,

Leaning back with authority,

With purpose,

Talking

To everyone

But me.

You caught my eye

As I passed you

Watching til I

Left your sight.

When I returned,

You had gone.

Stars crossing—

Swirling in a velvet

Summer sky

Falling to embrace

In a single

Glorious moment

Of joy

As in tenderness

I talk to you

And you,

You talk to me…

Living Dreams

Sweet rustle beneath my window

A night song

Soft and wild in the wind

Of tendrils climbing

Through thick weeds.

Vines breathing hard

Give life to the frosty rock

Emerging in secret

To thrive

Where some would struggle to grow

Among harsh stone

And heavy earth

Yet here,

Protected by moss

After the peace of rain

Only when the evening sun

Reflects the quiet murmur of spring

Sending a path of light

They bloom

Full flow

From every crevice

Between moistened rock

Thirsting in the moonlight

Listening in the shade

For the tune of summer

And the fruit of living dreams

Broken

(for my sister)

Broken,

Like sunlight through autumn leaves

Swirling in a tumult of color

And fury

Kicked up and matted when the

Cold silent rains

Pelt and whip.

Broken,

Like the last jagged yellow birch leaf

As the first snowflakes drift to

Swallow up the pain

Made in the USA
Middletown, DE
10 March 2023

26499794R00033